THE BEST IN

OFFICE INTERIOR

DESIGN

THE BEST IN

OFFICE INTERIOR

DESIGN

ALAN PHILLIPS

Batsford

A QUARTO BOOK

Published by B. T. Batsford Ltd.
4 Fitzhardinge Street
London W1H 0AH

ISBN 0–7134–7131–X

A catalogue record for this book is available from the British Library

This book was designed and produced by
Quarto Publishing plc
6 Blundell Street
London N7 9BH

Creative Director: Terry Jeavons
Designer: Wayne Blades
Editor: Viv Croot

Typeset in Great Britain by
Central Southern Typesetters, Eastbourne
Manufactured in Hong Kong by Excel Graphic Arts Ltd
Printed in Hong Kong by Leefung-Asco Printers Ltd

Contents

Introduction

Introduction

There are millions of people worldwide working in offices. For some, the office is a study attached to a private residence; for others, it is part of a huge conglomerate. Yet in spite of all the hours spent behind a desk, moving papers, typing and telephoning, it is only quite recently that the office building – and in particular the office interior – has come under the scrutiny of the architect.

A Radical Reappraisal

During the 1970s a reappraisal of the individual and collective workplace was promoted by moral, ethical and philosophical considerations in the cause of commercial advantage. Specialist advisers to large corporations began to establish a protocol for the organization of an office workforce. Comfort would lead to job satisfaction; job satisfaction would lead to increased productivity.

Comfort, however, was a general term comprising many specificities. In terms of arrangement, there were moves to take down the formica and aluminium partitions, allowing the workforce to emerge from the cellular office unit into the *bürolandschaft* or open plan system. Rather than a divisive environment reinforcing old hierarchies of power, the office became a community.

In support of these new communities, companies
provided crèches for the children of working parents,
swimming pools for exercise, well-equipped restaurants
and facilities where office-based associations, groups
and clubs could meet. Rather than employing an
anonymous office worker in an anonymous building
complex, the company was now playing host to
community life; the office became a working home-
from-home. Such a fundamental change in attitude
demanded a new direction in design.

**Willis, Faber & Dumas, Ipswich, Suffolk,
England**
Norman Foster's pioneering office building
incorporated a swimming pool, a manifestation
of the move to bring work and recreation
together under one roof in an attempt to
homogenize rather than compartmentalize the
office community.
ARCHITECT: Foster Associates, London, England

Johnson's Wax Building, Racine, Wisconsin, USA
Built in 1936, Frank Lloyd Wright's Johnson's Wax project made the quantum leap which set the paradigm for office design worldwide.
ARCHITECT: Frank Lloyd Wright

Johnson's Wax Building, Racine, Wisconsin, USA
Although 50 years old, the pyrex access tube linking one building to another creates a revolutionary aesthetic that has influenced many architects over the last four decades. The expression of light and structure through an illuminated canopy is contemporary to many buildings and office structures.
ARCHITECT: Frank Lloyd Wright

Pioneering Commissions: Johnson's Wax

The Johnson's Wax Company was a progenitor of the new awareness; in 1936 they commissioned Frank Lloyd Wright to design their new administration building at Racine, Wisconsin. The product was a devastating reappraisal of the workspace and its environment. The company had paid its staff the compliment of an office workplace by the hand of a great architect; at the same time, they proclaimed a corporate image for themselves that affirmed a commitment to development. The modern architecture of Wright was clean; the product was clean; and the publicity surrounding the innovative approach to office design and the exceptional quality of the architecture carried the name Johnson's Wax around the world.

The Second Wave: Centraal Beheer   But in the 1930s, this sort of experiment and patronage, albeit influential, was rare. It was not until the late 1960s that social experiment in office design began to be realized. In particular, Herman Hertzberger's Centraal Beheer building at Apeldoorn in the Netherlands, built 1968–1974, created a paradigm to reflect the moral and ethical values of a new consciousness. Like Wright's Johnson's Wax building 30 years earlier, the Centraal Beheer building established the protocol for an office community; and again, it was due to the client commissioning an architect of the very highest calibre. The product conferred a reputation on the company equal to the quality of the architecture.

And yet, notwithstanding some brilliant and notable exceptions, it took another 20 years before the relationship of eminent architect and office development became commonplace worldwide.

Centraal Beheer, Apeldoorn, Netherlands
In this famous example of the new work ethic of integration rather than segregation, the office is realised almost as a village or small town community, with 'streets' linking work stations, interior windows onto the streets, 'cornershop' refreshment stops and communal meeting places.
ARCHITECT: Herman Hertzberger, Amsterdam, Netherlands

The Broadgate Development, London, England
Quotations abound in the lobby of phase 7 of
the Broadgate Development at London's
Liverpool Street Terminus. The day-bed and table
are by Mies van der Rohe, lights are reminiscent
of the Viennese Secessionists and the floors and
walls belong to a Roman basilica. All are skilfully
composed in an heroic space, with sculpture
to suit.
ARCHITECT: Skidmore, Owings & Merrill,
London, England

Architecture In The Workplace   Rather than
cathedrals, city halls and landmark buildings in general, it
is now office building that is establishing the platforms of
excellence. Further, many architects whose manifestos
could once be pronounced only in the design of a rare
house for a rare client now have boundless opportunities
to express a polemical, ideological and theoretical
position within the programme of an office commission.

The banking tower has replaced the cathedral, the advertising agency has replaced the House. And it is not a case of radical corporations employing radical architects. The commercial lessons learnt from the Johnson's Wax and Centraal Beheer developments have been influential in two principal areas: firstly, that a good architect costs no more than a poor one; secondly, that good design pays.

Berrywood County Primary School, Hampshire, England
The Berrywood school declares a new optimism for educational buildings. With great skill, honed by strict budgets, the architects have established the new humanism that is becoming endemic across a range of public buildings, which like offices, were once the domain of ordinariness and mediocrity.
ARCHITECT: Hampshire County Architects Department, Winchester, Hampshire, England

The New Zeitgeist Furthermore, the architects' own offices have displayed an architectural nerve that visiting clients see as enhancing the productivity and goodwill of the office. There is a new catalogue of excellence from building types that, with some exceptions, were previously models of mediocrity. Schools in England and France are seen by critics as models of progressive theory and practice. Hospitals are being reappraised and redesigned to become paradigms of a new humanity. Banks, once bastions of conservatism, now exclaim a new radicalism.

In all, it would seem — as it is hoped — that the end of the twentieth century will be marked by a universal architectural adventure that will embrace the new *zeitgeist* as enthusiastically as did the artistic visionaries who began the revolt into modernism at the beginning of the century.

Central Bank, Vienna, Austria
The organic curves of the great sculptured hand which dominates Gunther Domenig's Viennese banking hall brings a touch of humanity into the hard bright world of the money market.
ARCHITECT: Gunther Domenig, Vienna, Austria

The Cook-Fort Worth Children's Medical Center, Fort Worth, Texas, USA
Fairytale towers and ice-cream colours make the Center an attractive, entertaining and intriguing place, a welcoming haven for sick or nervous children.
ARCHITECT: David M. Schwarz Architectural Services, Washington DC, USA

Chiat Day Advertising, London, England
Dynamic, energetic and unencumbered by
irrelevant historicity, this interior's success is the
result of carefully and meticulously planned
geometries.
ARCHITECT : Stephano de Martino, London,
England

Traditional

In common with the word 'modern', 'traditional' can mean many things. In the context of office design, it is understood to represent an approach that employs methods, materials, idiomatic devices, styles and architectural languages that belong clearly to an historical-architectural period substantially pre-dating the second half of the twentieth century.

In office programmes that call for the re-use of an historically fragile building that is itself of architectural importance, traditional will mean a proposal of restoration and conservation. When a client calls for a scheme that recalls an historical period, or commissions a building in the manner of another period or style, traditional may mean Revivalist. Both cases call upon a high degree of scholarship from the architect in order to distinguish themselves from pastiche and parody.

Over the last 20 years, new building programmes, especially in office projects, have derived an aesthetic from the process of building a contemporary structural and servicing system, and then laying over with cladding elements culled from various historical periods and styles. These quotations from history are often mixed to provide stylistic collages and bizarre compositions tending towards eclecticism. By the interrelationship of stylistic fragments, some architects enjoy the wit that can be promoted by the mixing of metaphors, meanings, codes and semiotics traditionally associated with the historical elements of the composition.

The danger is that, if a piece of architecture is asked to be read, it can so often be misread if the language reveals a miscellany of interpretations. The same can be said of ornament and decoration. Much of the quality of a traditional view of architecture rests in the scholarship of its making. Ornament is as deeply rooted in theory as are the more abstract phenomena of architecture. Without a view or understanding of these theories, decorative and ornamental devices can become gratuitous and wilful.

 ▼  ▼  ▼

Massachusetts Financial Services Company, Boston, Massachusetts, USA

This company entertains clients frequently so the executive floor features extra wide corridors suitable for functions. The conference room table can be separated into smaller tables for dining. This dining space is augmented by a series of private dining rooms. Custom designed mahogany millwork gives the floor a richness and warmth.

ARCHITECT: Jung/Brannen, Boston, Massachusetts, USA

Gilliam and Company Inc., New York City, New York, USA

In office refurbishment programmes that are either conversions of old buildings or new buildings in revivalist styles, great attention has to be paid to detailing and craftsmanship. The Gilliam project is a state-of-the-art example with an almost Baroque mixture of wallings, floor finishes and lighting assemblies that comprise a rich decorative interior.

ARCHITECT: The Switzer Group Inc., New York City, New York, USA

Cavelti Capital, Toronto, Ontario, Canada
Strongly figured and richly grained timberwork
marks routeways and entrances. Floors exploit
changes of surface and texture and grey walls
act as a foil to lighting systems and artworks.
ARCHITECT: Inger Bartlett and Associates
Limited, Toronto, Ontario, Canada

Perkins Coie, Seattle, Washington, USA
A neutral palette with varying finish textures
forms a clean and elegant backdrop for the
client's (a law firm) extensive art collection.
Dramatic views of Puget Sound and the Cascade
Mountains complement the monochromatic
finishes, accentuated by bold use of colour
Natural materials include French limestone,
beech wood and glass.
ARCHITECT: Gensler Associates, San Francisco,
California, USA

Crown American Corporate Office Building, Johnstown, Pennsylvania, USA

The boardroom takes advantage of the full value of polished timber which simultaneously reflects and absorbs light. The purpose-made carpets and furniture of the Vice President's office are in contrast to plain white walls that are marked out in stone coursings to imply solidity.

ARCHITECT: Michael Graves, Princeton, New Jersey, USA

505 Montgomery, San Francisco, California, USA

A contrast of light materials, texture and engraved decoration provides an engaging richness to the entrance of these offices.

ARCHITECT: Skidmore, Owings & Merrill, New York, USA

Nikko Securities Headquarters, London, England

The entrance is distinguished by the prominent placing of the company logo and the banded relationship of steel and stone. In contrast to the permanence of the external stone facings and entrance steps, the interior is soft and warm.

ARCHITECT: McColl, London, England

Heron International, London, England

The brief for the external and internal refurbishment of these offices called for a design that was hardwearing and long lasting, with rich English qualities. Predominantly natural materials were chosen, with a combination of oak and granite extensively used. Purpose designed furniture was also commissioned. The principal corridor is finished in browns and creams with recessed ceiling lighting dropping puddles of light at entrance ways and illuminating wallpaintings.

ARCHITECT: The Design Solution, London, England

London Dock House, London, England
The interior space in this office refurbishment programme is homogenized with painted walls and ceilings. The glazed rooflight provides directions at high level, while the floor lighting system amplifies the perspective. The heating radiators illustrate the difficulty of integrating services into an historical building.
ARCHITECT: Thomas Brent Associates, London, England

Queen Anne Building, London, England

This splendid Queen Anne house in Chandos
Place was refurbished as a speculative office
development. It has been returned to its former
glory, using traditional quality materials.
However, the staircase has a contemporaneity
that respects the volume of the interior without
patronizing the history of the host building.
ARCHITECT: McColl, London, England

Ellerbe Becket Inc, St Paul, Minnesota, USA
Located in the Minnesota World Trade Center,
Ellerbe Becket's St Paul office blends classic and
contemporary design elements. All the principal
spaces enjoy a relationship between natural and
artificial light. Vaulted ceilings, textured columns
and pilasters, tiled floors, and finely detailed
furniture combine to provide a rich office interior
that is at once diverse and homogenous.
ARCHITECT: Ellerbe Becket Inc, St Paul,
Minnesota, USA

3 Stratford Place, Mayfair, London, England
Classicism borders on baroque in this Mayfair
interior; office seems to humble a word for it.
Rigorous attention to the authenticity of the
colours and the dominance of the scintillating
chandeliers, which are contemporary features of
the original Georgian house, successfully dispels
any distant shadow of kitsch.
ARCHITECT: DY Davies Associates, Richmond,
Surrey, England

Seward Properties, Stratten Street, London, England

This Mayfair townhouse, built in 1897 is a Grade II listed building. The refurbishment included a conservatory in the lightwell and an extra level on the roof.

ARCHITECT: The Design Solution, London, England

Pacific Telesis, San Francisco, California, USA
The conference room is characterized by an enormous table. As well as accommodating its function, it serves to reflect the geometries of the ceiling which, by its concavity, offers concealed ambient lighting. The richness of the space is created by the inscription of various timber veneers which capitalize on the quality of natural materials to reflect and soften the spot and task lighting systems.
ARCHITECT: Skidmore, Owings & Merrill, San Francisco, California, USA

South East Bank, Miami, Florida, USA
The simple repetition of three internal windows against a series of monochromatic space dividers creates an unusually dynamic contrast of solid and void. Concealed lighting is used to great effect.

ARCHITECT: Skidmore, Owings & Merrill

▼

▼

▼

Modern Vernacular

Beyond a programmatic response to the demands of a brief, the architect has a duty to recognize and respond to the cultural inheritance implied in the subject of the programme, as well as the cultural inheritance embodied in the history and geography of the building's context.

These are vernacular considerations; but vernacular does not mean a type of architectural apeing of past regionalized styles. Because vernacular is a process, part of a passing-on, there is an integrity of intention, an honesty and truthfulness that embodies an essence or quality that, although abstract, can be translated in such a way as to reflect the memory of the process and fragments of the products. For example, Nicoll Russell's bank has a Scottishness to its architectural language through the quotation of a vernacular geometry.

Modern Vernacular architecture is not referential for its own sake: it is a process by which a modernism is established within the tradition of development on which the meaning of vernacular should properly depend. The multispoked wheel of the MG sports car is a Modern vernacular, embracing a traditionally developed figure with a contemporary technology. In different ways, RSCG Conran, Fitzroy Robinson, and MJP Architects have each established a contemporariness from the production of an architectural language in response to the culture of the object beside the culture of the subject.

**Butlers' Wharf Development Corporation,
London, England**
The warehouses in this development date from
late Victorian period. The brief was to retain or
re-use original materials and existing details.
Office spaces are defined by gridded glass block
screens that offer privacy as well as
transparency. Polished timber floors reflect
natural light with a richness that is traditional to
London riverside warehouse buildings. The
furniture is robust, also following in the tradition
of wharf buildings.
ARCHITECT: RSCG Conran Design Limited,
London, England

Mitsui Trust & Banking Co Ltd, London, England

The corporate headquarters for Mitsui in the Broadgate development accommodates up to 200 people. As the design evolved it moved away from the traditional English style to a more Japanese feel. Woodwork, furniture and screens were all specially made to simple designs from limed oak, marble and etched glass; work surfaces are of linoleum.

ARCHITECT: Fitzroy Robinson Partnership, London, England

TSB Bank plc, St Andrews, Fife, Scotland
This award-winning project is typical of Nicoll Russell Studios' work, which takes great care over the selection and relationship of materials and pays meticulous attention to detail. The bank's traditional claim to the high street has been exaggerated through the transparency of the façade and the openness of the interior. Natural daylight mixes with task lighting to animate the interior.
ARCHITECT: Nicoll Russell Studios, Dundee, Scotland

Modern   With the revolution in information
technology, computer systems, fax, video fax and tele
communications, the office is a model of modernity.

All the technical systems by which the commercial office
maintains a competitive edge within the world market
can be directly related to theories and ideologies of the

Modern movement and Internationalism. Reyner Banham correlated the relationship of theory and design after the Industrial Revolution and through modern history to what he described as the First Machine Age; the microchip and communication technology have promulgated the Second Machine Age; Virtual Reality and the tele-commuter might make Third. All combine to provide the contemporary architect with a design response compatible to the creative inventiveness and energy of systems development.

Most major corporations together with the smallest offices have found it natural and inevitable to combine a modern technology with a modern aesthetic. If the word 'modern' has been too ill-defined or prone to misinterpretation of theoretical definition, it may be better to say that architects have been encouraged to establish a language of technological contemporariness that provides *inter alia* for systems of structure, services and materials that are as sophisticated as the operations they are designed to protect.

This Modernism, however, is not slavishly bonded to an enforcing ideology. It is more liberal and able to take advantage of contemporary materials or radical inventions for traditional materials. Further, contemporary geometry is seen as more elastic than traditional geometry. Orthodoxies are being challenged to provide an architecture of dynamic, delight and duality.

DIN, London, England

DIN is a new corporate identity for a high quality
hi-fi specialist. The interior is finished in silver
sand rendered walls, a jarra floor and panels
wrapped in pleated artist's linen behind the
product display. An illuminated glass staircase
leads to the basement demonstration room.
ARCHITECT: Paul Mullins Associates, London,
England

Jestico + Whiles Offices, London, England

By careful extension and alteration, the underused resource of the existing building, a dilapidated four-storey industrial warehouse, has been transformed to provide a practical workplace which reflects the occupants' aims and contributes sympathetically to the regeneration of the locality. The building was totally reorganized to increase space; the top two floors are extended to provide a linked double-height workspace to enable all design and support groups to operate in one area. Throughout the design, materials and components reflect the designer's interest in the use of lightweight and economical off-the-peg industrial sections and components.

ARCHITECT: Jestico + Whiles, London, England

afa Asset Services Inc., New York City, New York, USA

In an attempt to address the difficult problems posed by the renovation of a space which contained both stylistic and inherited programmatic problems, the architects turned to the tradition of great New York commercial building of the earlier part of the century. The design was concerned with the people who inhabited and used the place – design tenants and their clients, visitors, service personnel and the general public. The intention was for the lobby to function as an animated pedestrian street, a gesture towards giving a public face to what is essentially a private office building lobby.

ARCHITECT: P. Michael Marino, Marino Newman Architects, New York City, New York, USA

IBM Midlands Marketing Centre, Warwick, Warwickshire, England

This design provides a comfortable and humane working environment for 500 or so staff. Everyone has a view either of the landscaped court or the surrounding countryside. In the open traffic areas, the main elements are the work stations and the storage walls arranged at right angles to the external façade. These divide the office space into bays, which are further defined by a demountable screen system especially developed for the project. Lighting levels are under individual control which can override the general office lighting.

ARCHITECT: Rock Townsend, London, England

Design House, London, England

In this scheme, a disused car showroom was transformed into a design studio. The steel frame structure of the existing building was altered to create double volume studio space within the existing envelope. Externally, the existing cladding was removed and replaced with a combination of insulated aluminium panels and large glazed areas. The glass wall is laid between a row of muscular leaning columns

ARCHITECT: Troughton McCaslan, London, England

3i, London, England

An arrangement of simple geometries clearly
articulates this double-height space. Colour in
fabrics and screens has been carefully selected to
mark out different functional areas.

ARCHITECT: Peter Leonard Associates, London,
England

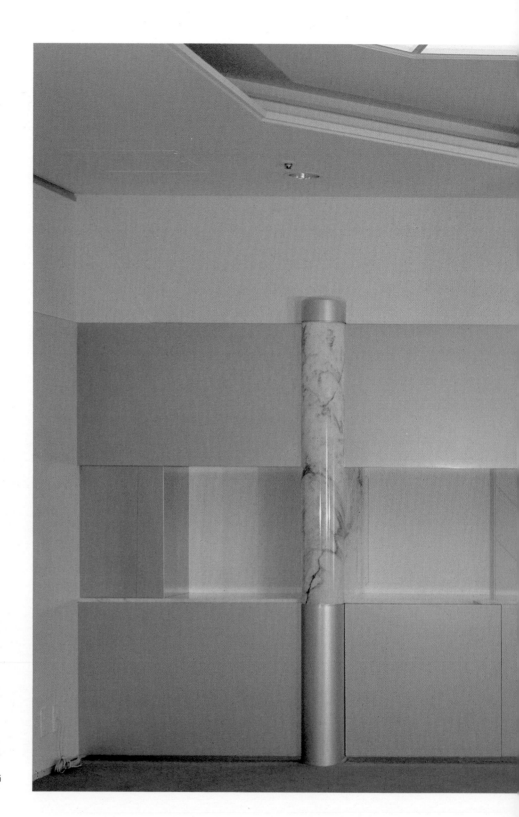

Wacoal Kojimachi Building, Tokyo, Japan
The eave-awning extending over the main entranceway calls down a flying saucer, a brief visitor from the world of the future, while on the wall immediately opposite the entrance, a mirrored stainless steel sculpture by Tada Minami casts a distorted reflection from the past. In the elevator hall, the floor depicts an age-old geomantic symbol in a mosaic of marble gathered from the countries along the Silk Road. In the President's room, the walls are cut out and indented and composed around a polygonal lantern light.
ARCHITECT: Kisho Kurakawa Architects & Associates, Tokyo, Japan

Wacoal Kojimachi continued over page

Wacoal Kojimachi Building, Tokyo, Japan
The guest house/reception room on the ninth floor of the lingerie company building overlooks the Imperial Palace; it comprises a variety of geometries layered and interlocked and seemingly well-supported by one central stainless steel column. Sliding Japanese *fusuma* screens make the boundary to the room the only indication of scale.

ARCHITECT: Kisho Kurokawa Architects and Associates, Tokyo, Japan

Heian Kojimachi Building, Tokyo, Japan
The building consists basically of two elements:
the entrance area and the office area. These two
elements are in symbiosis while retaining their
own shapes and spaces suitable for each of
them. The entrance which has triangular
penthouse on the top, and a semicircular
aluminium wall and a polished granite wall on
the sides, has two zones: upper, including part
of the office areas on the third and fourth floor,
and lower which is a void space over the
entrance proper. On the west wall, glass blocks
framed in aluminium are set in flamed granite
cladding pillars and beams. The aluminium
panels can be opened to provide natural
ventilation. In the afternoon, 150 gold plates
encased in the glass blocks glint in the sunlight.
ARCHITECT: Kisho Kurokawa Architects and
Associates, Tokyo, Japan

Capita Centre, Sydney, NSW, Australia
All the office floors are free from internal columns, which are often used to characterize repetitive cellular spaces. A greater emphasis is therefore placed on lighting patterns, furniture placement and artworks. This is particularly important for the deep plan internal sections of the building that cannot enjoy the ground-floor public thoroughfare and glass-roofed galleria or views over the city of Sydney.
ARCHITECT: Harry Seidler & Associates, Milson's Point, NSW Australia

Aon Corporation, Chicago, Illinois, USA
The boardroom is located on the top floor of a
new 30-storey building. The grain, texture,
figure and colour of Macassar and Gaboon
ebony have been exploited to frame the principal
table. The wall panels are toplit which has the
effect of lightening the ceiling and causing
timber to appear to darken as it meets the floor.
ARCHITECT: Larson Associates, Chicago, Illinois,
USA

Starkmann Library Services, London, England
The directors' offices and ancillary spaces are the products of a rigorous theoretical base that is rooted in the Minimalist school. The architect must be in control of every surface, since such a disciplined control of space, plane, form and surface cannot afford the sort of errors that can sometimes be disguised in more random architectral adventures.
ARCHITECT: Pawson Silvestrin, London, England

Pacific Bell, San Ramon, California, USA
Toplighting draws attention to the principal office space which is animated by huge mushroom-shaped columns. The relationship of natural light, structure and artificial light characterizes and gives scale to the working environment.
ARCHITECT: Skidmore, Owings & Merrill, Los Angeles, California, USA

The Lloyds Building, London, England

The Lloyds building is principally distinguished by the huge atrium through which escalators provide vertical circulation to the open plan offices on either side. The proportions of the central space, together with the shape of the end windows have led critics to describe the building as 'cathedral of work'. Lifts are exquisitely detailed, as is the entrance canopy and exterior glazing systems.

ARCHITECT: Richard Rogers Partnership, London, England

Shell House, Melbourne, Victoria, Australia
The 23 levels of offices above the main lobby and entrance comprise a double curve, maximizing views, rationalizing structure and optimizing the energy requirements of the building. The executive suites on the upper floors are cut back and then connected vertically with staircases that embody the geometry of the external skin of the building. Lighting grids further amplify the geometrical figure of the internal partitions.
ARCHITECT: Harry Seidler & Associates, Milson's Point, NSW, Australia

Grosvenor Place, Sydney, NSW, Australia
The plan of the tower building is a double curve configuration, maximizing views across Sydney Opera House to the harbour. The geometry is carried inside the offices to reflect in partition systems, furniture and lighting layouts.
ARCHITECT: Harry Seidler & Associates, Milson's Point, NSW, Australia

Municipal Nursery, Paris, France
Splashes of colour provide a counterpoint to
walls that are otherwise painted surfaces, all clad
in horizontal timber panelling. Together, they
form an almost painterly composition, especially
when illuminated by the relatively flat light of
utility striplights and supported by small section
circular steel columns.
ARCHITECT: Marc Beri and Phillippe Gazeau,
Paris, France

Industrial Kitchen, Paris, France

A narrow cut between access corridor and a tall, vertiginous wall is rooflit to wash light into the lower areas of the building. This cut provides a vertical foil against the horizontal access corridors that pass through finely detailed and elegant steel-framed glass thresholds.

ARCHITECT: Phillipe Gazeau, Paris, France

Enron Corporation, Houston, Texas, USA
Through overlapping geometries and subtle changes in the surface texture of materials and colour, the architects have created a spatial layering that accentuates both the horizontal and the vertical dimensions and frames distant views to the outside. Polished timber floor surfaces and doors promote this device.

ARCHITECT: Gensler Associates, San Francisco, California, USA

Hampton House, London, England
Reflective surfaces combined with highly
polished and mirrored screens shift the
perspective of the small reception area. The floor
beneath the reception desk seems to be carried
through the solid and leads the eye of the visitor
to the point of enquiry.
ARCHITECT: McColl, London, England

Delaney Fletcher Slaymaker Delaney Bozell, London, England

DFSDB was formed from the merger of two smaller advertising agencies who had hitherto worked out of separate buildings. The floor plan acknowledges the two aspects of the company's activities, creative work and administration. These were given expression by the creation of two long walls, one curving and oak sheathed, the other straight and tiled in glass mosaic. These lead towards the two departments, changes in materials and the sequence of public and semi-public spaces creating a multicentric spatial hierarchy.

ARCHITECT: Harper MacKay, London, England

NEXT, Enderby, Leicestershire, England
The simple plan provides room for expansion
and change with minimal disruption. The
concept of 'mock shops' within the building
conveys corporate objectives at a glance to City
financiers and staff alike. Decks, bridges and
staircases span a central atrium space and serve
smaller cellular offices. The light steel and timber
structures counterpoint solid masonry walls.
Natural light spilling through a steel and glass
canopy creates random shadows, adding
another layer of interest.
ARCHITECT: ORMS, London, England

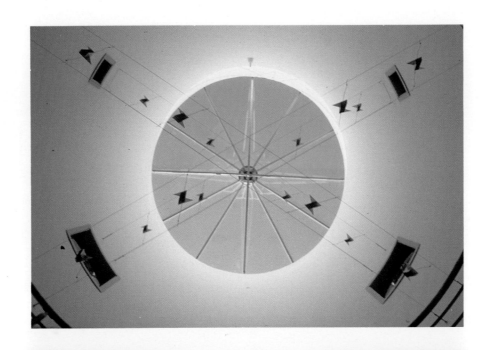

Next HQ continued over page

Next HQ continued

Romantic Language Building, Yale University, New Haven, Connecticut, USA

Four separate historic rowhouses have been interconnected to accommodate faculty offices and seminar rooms. Ground floor entrances are threaded between existing retail shops. A compact skylit atrium has been created on the upper levels to orient visitors and introduce natural light to the building. Apses, balconies and material and surfaces of the original structure enliven long corridors.

ARCHITECT: Allan Dehar Associates, New Haven, Connecticut, USA

La Grande Arche, Paris, France
The construction of the great arched office complex largely dominates and determines the aesthetics of the interior spaces, with relatively light glazed curtain walls set in contrast to concrete cellular structural floors and ceilings.
ARCHITECT: Otto von Spreckelson

Royal Bank, Toronto, Ontario, Canada
Suspended steel and glass canopies against a combination of reflective surfaces highlighted by task and spot lights create a delicate composition within the principal space, which is layered both vertically and horizontally to provide visual depth. The lower banking area involves several layers of design objectives: the architectural reference to the banking hall upstairs, the consideration for interior public space accessing adjacent buildings and subways; and the banking function. Conspicuous segregation of public space is achieved through the use of stainless steel space frame designed to direct people through the public corridor to their various destinations.
ARCHITECT: Inger Bartlett and Associates Limited, Toronto, Ontario, Canada

Kirkland & Ellis, Denver, Colorado, USA
The offices are distinguished by a principal
staircase which is lit from above. Metal and glass
create an assembly of reflections that are in
contrast to the more cellular spaces that
surround the circulation space.
ARCHITECT: Skidmore, Owings & Merrill, Chicago,
Illinois, USA

Willis, Faber & Dumas, Ipswich, Suffolk, England

Steel, water and glass and light creates an extraordinary ground floor to this office building. Although the ceiling is relatively low for a swimming pool, the carefully figured dimensions of the space and the glazed-in wall combine to provide an interior which is unusual to swimming pool places. Although the building is now listed as being of architectural interest, the pool might still be filled in if the owners proceed with their office expansion programme.

ARCHITECT: Foster Associates, London, England

T. L. Horton Design Inc., Dallas, Texas, USA
The variation in lighting gives depth and drama
to an otherwise traditional arrangement of wall,
staircase, screen and floor. Task and spot lighting
accentuate architectural scenarios and lead the
eye from circulation spaces to office interiors.
ARCHITECT: T. L. Horton Design Inc., Dallas, Texas,
USA

T. L. Horton continued

T. L. Horton Design, Dallas, Texas, USA
The principal offices, marked out by a number of
partitions forming simple white cubic screens,
are capped by a white steel and glass canopy
which creates the impression of a building within
a building. Lighting serves to reinforce the
abstract quality of the office interior.

ARCHITECT: T. L. Horton Design, Dallas, Texas,
USA

The Riverside Centre, Brisbane, NSW, Australia
The Riverside Centre comprises a huge
development with extensive landscaping
proposals. Despite the scale of the office tower,
attention to detail throughout the interior is
exquisite, with meticulous assemblies of colour,
natural materials, light and texture.
ARCHITECT: Harry Seidler Associate, Milson's
Point, NSW, Australia

American Express Bank International, Beverly Hills, California, USA

A traditional interior to a small and elegant space housing private banking offices; these are connected by a glass enclosed serpentine staircase to additional offices on another floor. This relatively small staircase is carefully lit and screened and the main reception area is characterized by the precise placing of furniture, flowers and artworks. Natural light is brought into the interior space by deep light wells. The space is enriched by sycamore panelling with mahogany inlays. A series of landscaped terraces provides opportunity for casual outdoor entertainment of clients.

ARCHITECT: Gensler Associates, San Francisco, California, USA

F 1 Group, Hemel Hempstead, Hertfordshire, England

A timber floor acts as a horizontal canvas on which desk, carpet, steel support columns and lighting grids work in counterpoint. Colour is principally created through the reflection of natural materials.

ARCHITECT: Crabtree Hall, London, England

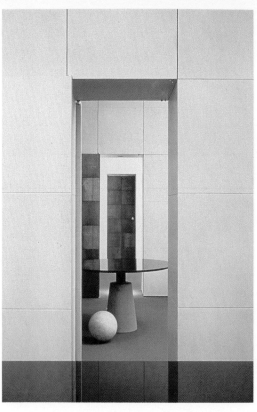

Vignelli Associates, New York City, New York, USA

Vignelli's design for their own Manhattan offices was intended to express the company philosophy on two and three dimensional design. This project was a testing ground for new ideas. Much of the exploration concerns ordinary materials applied in extraordinary ways: furniture from crude steel sheets and tubes straight from the factory; walls and doors covered with sheets of hand-waxed lead; gold leaf applied to industrial steel tubing used as a table base; particle board, stained white and lacquered used like fine wood to panel office walls and construct work stations. Each base has its own specificity of form and function. Details, colours, lighting and texture are appropriate to changing requirements and atmospheres. Perspective is used with great care as is the relationship between ambient, task and spot lighting to amplify spatial sequences.

ARCHITECT: Vignelli Associates, New York City, New York, USA

Museum Showroom and Theatre for Poltrona Frau, Tolentino, Italy

Furniture and screens are carefully composed against simple walls and floors to create the maximum impact from minimum means. The same dynamic simplicity is employed in the external spaces, with the only diagonals created by light and shade.

ARCHITECT: Vignelli Associates, New York City, New York, USA

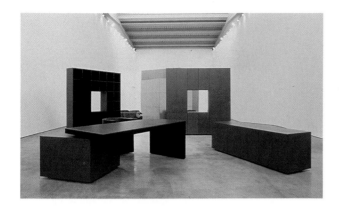

Poltrona Frau continued

Offices for Museum Showroom and Theatre for Poltrona Frau, Tolentino, Italy

This is a beautiful space of extraordinary scale and simplicity. The boundary of the space is marked out with task and spot lighting. The floor and walls are passive surfaces against which furniture and exhibits can rest with prominence. The ceiling exaggerates the composition of the interior space.

ARCHITECT: Vignelli Associates, New York City, New York, USA

A. J. Vines, London, England

The offices of a firm of marketing consultants were converted from part of a former Victorian prison for women. Particular concerns included the provision of functional flexible space with sunlight, shade, colour, sparkle, energy efficient performance; quality of environment was considered paramount. A circular panel in the form of a fish-eye lens reflects the rooflit offices with light skeletal steel structures and white walls throughout. Vision panels to access doors are borrowed from the nautical technologies.
ARCHITECT: Weston Williamson, London, England

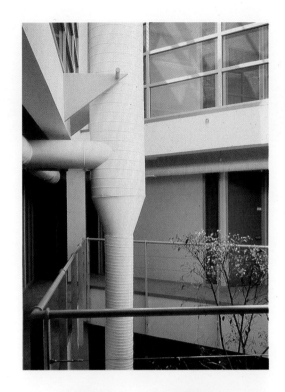

Policy Studies Institute, London, England

The five storey building, brick on a steel frame, was built in the 1920s; its plane shape, a wedge tapering from 25m to virtually nothing, presented a particular challenge. The research offices are grouped around a triple volume atrium which links the top three floors of the building. The atrium resolves problems of lighting, ventilation and heating posed by deep space offices and also provides a 'healthy building'.

ARCHITECT: Jestico + Whiles, London, England

Ove Arup & Partners, London, England
The offices, constructed in steel and glass, are distinguished by the quality of light allowed into the interiors and the sense of perspective created along the principal spaces. A sense of calm prevails, in contrast to the business of the city outside, which seeks to prove the appropriateness of traditional industrial materials to modern office interiors.
ARCHITECT: Jestico + Whiles, London, England

Imagination Headquarters, London, England
The principal circulation space sits between two existing buildings and is covered by a lightweight tensile fabric structure engineered by Buro Happold. Ten finely detailed lightweight steel and aluminium bridges span the two buildings, creating a layered dynamic. The quality of light that passes through the translucent fabric roof canopy holds the composition together and is evenly reflected by the white-painted walls of the existing converted buildings.
ARCHITECT: Herron Associates, London, England

ORMS, London, England

The entrance to the architects' own offices is distinguished by powerful graphics and a finely detailed door. The complexity of the door gives way to an elegant simplicity, comprising plain white surfaces, glazed screens and highly reflective floors.

ARCHITECT: ORMS, London, England

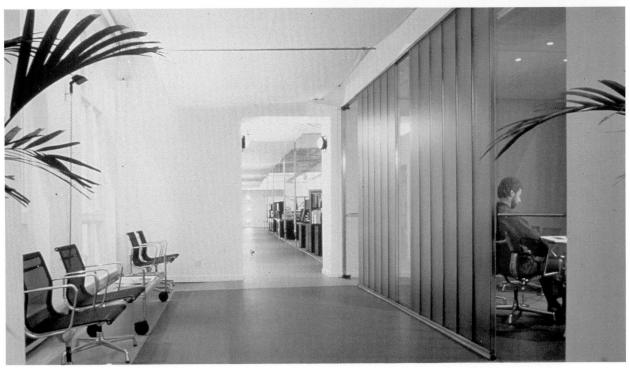

Deloitte & Touche, Wilton, Connecticut, USA
Working within the unusual geometry of an
existing Roche Dinkeloo building, the design
incorporates diverse uses: TV studios, training
facilities and administration areas. The
centrepiece is a huge executive area with
reception/gallery space, boardroom and senior
partner offices. Some of the principal pieces of
furniture are heroic in scale and in a minimal
office landscape become sculptural in their
isolation. Various metals are used to distinguish
joints and junctions, with the inherent properties
of these materials used to create richness in an
otherwise simple composition. Canopies of
natural light mark out specific areas of
importance to provide further activity and
interest through shadow making.
ARCHITECT: Ellerbe, Becket Inc, New York City,
New York, USA

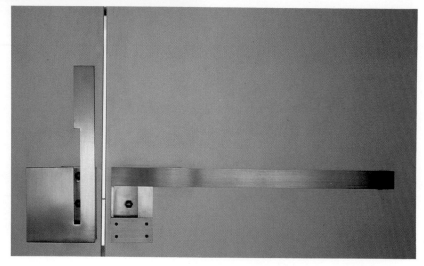

Deloitte & Touche continued over page

Deloitte & Touche continued

Deloitte & Touche, Wilton, Connecticut, USA
The interrelationship of natural light artificial
light, materials and textures brought together in
sometimes very abstract compositions creates an
office complex of extraordinary richness. Details
are very carefully composed. The longer vistas,
by contrast, are painterly, especially those under
natural light.
ARCHITECT: Ellerbe Becket Inc, New York City,
New York, USA

Ellerbe Becket, Kansas City, Missouri, USA

The Kansas City offices are distinguished by the relationship between natural light, artificial light and the composition of materials that comprise this complex of offices. In particular, spotlighting and task lighting have been used to distinguish set pieces of office furniture and equipment. Various materials both reflect and absorb light to create a continuously changing officescape.

ARCHITECT: Ellerbe Becket Inc, Kansas City, Missouri, USA

Ellerbe Becket continued over page

Ellerbe Becket Kansas City continued

Ellerbe Becket, Kansas City, Missouri, USA
Office partitions are cut into abstract cubic geometries that create variety between one unit and another. Furniture and accessories are finely detailed with harmonies created through contrasting materials. Colour is passive in general, with specific points of interest distinguished by the richness of natural materials.
ARCHITECT: Ellerbe Becket Inc, Kansas City, Missouri, USA

Della Femina McNamee Inc., New York City, New York, USA

The offices for this advertizing agency occupy the top three floors and the newly constructed penthouse of a former loft building. A feature is the large, sculptural light steel stairway that rises from the ground floor and gives access to the various offices above. In contrast, the steel and glass framing the partitions on the upper floors employ a simple modesty. Throughout, artificial light has been carefully devised to create an engaging contrast between the principal elements of the architectural composition.

ARCHITECT: Beyer Blinder Belle, New York City, New York, USA

Herman Miller Showroom, Chicago, Illinois, USA

The reception desk to the office area of the showroom is spotlit and counterpointed against a heavily textured wall that acts as a foil to the principal circulation space. This is marked by a grid of huge columns clad in stainless steel to reflect natural and artificial light.

ARCHITECT: Skidmore, Owings & Merrill, Chicago, Illinois, USA

The Clove Building, London, England

The Clove Building is a dockside warehouse, renovated and converted to provide office space on the upper floors, with shops and parking at ground level. Selective demolition of the original building created a central lightwell, to bring light into the deep plan spaces of the upper office floors. The regular grid of the existing structure is abandoned on the top floor, where the wide spans of the new roof are supported on a minimum of slender circular columns. The top floor offices open out onto terraces behind the framework of the concrete facade.

ARCHITECT: Allies and Morrison, London, England

The Scott Howard Building, London, England

The new building replicates the original structure of a church which originally occupied the site. The front elevation is a reconstructed façade of stucco and solid brickwork. The brickwork becomes a skin which wraps around the other three sides of the building and encloses the separate structure of the offices. There is a double height space between office and façade. This space is reiterated above, where the office floors open out onto a two-storey atrium. A huge west-facing window further emphasizes the distinction between the deeply modelled church façade and the modern white interior.

ARCHITECT: Allies and Morrison, London, England

Foster Associates, London, England
The entrance and reception area is a passive
space, devoid of the structural elements that
comprise so much of Norman Foster's signature.
The engineering vocabulary, evident in the Hong
Kong and Shanghai banks, for example, is here
reduced and condensed to the reception table
which remains as an icon to the aesthetic values
of the practice.
ARCHITECT: Foster Associates, London, England

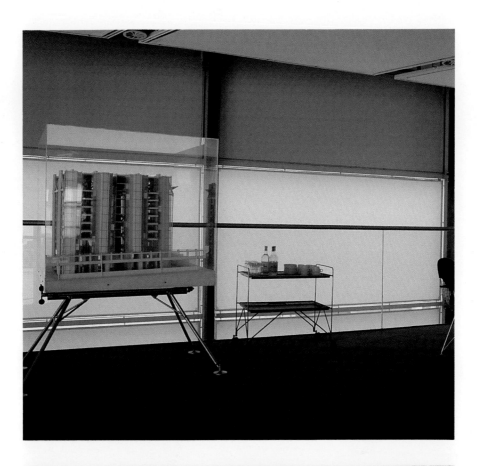

Jessica Square, London, England

Jessica Square office development is a shell and core speculative operation, but of a quality rarely seen in Europe. Further, the architects have distinguished what could legitimately have been passed by as an ordinary building within a strict cost-control mandate. The office interiors are passive and await the personalities of the incoming tenants. However, the common areas, including warehouses and circulation spaces, have been detailed with great care and sophisticaion to include materials such as Welsh slate and American oak. Moreover, the building is healthy. Rather than relying on air-conditioning for the deep plan office configuration, the narrow plan of a bifurcated building mass allows for natural ventilation via pivoting louvres, natural light and intimate views onto a private courtyard.

ARCHITECT: Munkenbeck and Marshall, London, England

Jessica Square continued over page

Jessica Square continued

Battery Park City Financial Center, New York City, New York, USA

As parts of large inner city commercial development, offices sometimes have two interiors. At Battery Park, a huge interior space or urban refuge is captured under a glazed atrium to form a winter garden. Inside this envelope sit the offices, with 'external' windows addressing an 'internal' court. It can be argued that the arrangement of sunlight and daylight is an improvement over the conventional condition of external window to the outside world.

ARCHITECT: Cesar Pelli, New Haven, Connecticut, USA

Bridge Studios, London, England

Bridge Studios are housed in a two-storey steel framed building composed of two overlapping golden section rectangles. The elegant simplicity of the structure and the transparency of the fabric lets the interior reveal itself after dark and be reflected by day. The building is a statement on Modernism, in sharp contrast to the Baroque vocabulary of nearby Hammersmith Bridge.

ARCHITECT: Manser Associates, London, England

Town End House, Havant Council Offices, Havant, Hampshire, England
The core offices are ranged around and look into a vaulted hall, formalized by two rows of columns that take the eye to and from a large glazed screen, and a small garden beyond. The space is layered horizontally and vertically by structure and fabric to animate a modest and beautifully articulated geometrical composition, all of which is framed and contained by the circle.
ARCHITECT: MacCormack, Jamieson and Pritchard, London, England

Offices for Trattoria Capri, Plymouth, Devonshire, England

The office entrance is marked out by a double curve of glass blocks, a terrazzo column and translucent glazed wall tiles. Inside, the reception desk rests on huge stone spheres with solid sheets of terrazzo supported by weight and gravity. Lighting is provided by a mixture of neon, ultraviolet and fluorescent tubes.

ARCHITECT: Alan Phillips Associates, Brighton, East Sussex, England

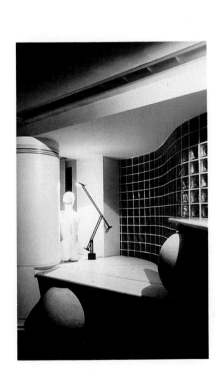

The Fitzpatrick Building, London, England

This is a refurbishment of an existing corner site, a two-storey factory enclosed by warehousing and terraced housing. Large windows provide interaction at street level and the entrance is set back on the corner below a curved metal and glass tower. The tower culminates in an oval boardroom on the sixth floor, with a glazed perimeter to the offices around it allowing panaramic views of the city. The main offices have floor-to-ceiling glazing facing the enclosed garden, which covers the ground level car park.

ARCHITECT: Chassay Architects, London, England

Bank of China, Hong Kong

The principal lobby to the banking hall has clearly expressed the geography of the building. To amplify the route from the ground plane, a huge kite-shaped void has been quarried out of the ceiling as a focus for the elevator. Polished stone exaggerates the precise internal geometries and floor lighting encourages direction.

ARCHITECT: Pei Cobb Freed & Partners, New York City, New York, USA

Century Tower, Tokyo, Japan

The heroic structure provides an ordering system
for the building's interior. Scale is distorted at
one level and then restored through a landscape
of leather furniture and a conventional door.
Through a layering of glazing system and
overlapped geometries, reflections create a
distorted cubic composition that is in
counterpoint to the sophisticated articulation of
the major spaces.

ARCHITECT: Foster Associates, London, England

Century Tower continued over page

Century Tower continued

New Modern

Only in retrospect and by historical contextual analysis can a group or movement be categorized and properly defined. Only after a lengthy period of time has elapsed is it possible to conclude that an object or movement or group of architects were, in their time, *avant-garde.*

▼

▼

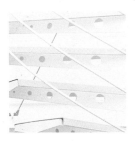

▼

And yet, new work that is contemporary and therefore *zeitgeistlich,* difficult to define or categorize, or is radical enough to be beyond definition is too easily labelled *avant-garde.*

But there is a New Modern. Architects and designers are emerging to take Modern principles only as the starting point for their work. Thereafter, the architectural ideas and elements are rearranged, distorted, fractured, reorientated and deconstructed to create an architectural grammar and syntax that directly confronts and challenges modern orthodoxies, principles and controlling ideologies.

Whereas this work is often found in clubs, bars, restaurants and those building types where temporality will limit the risk of sustained offence, many of the New Modern architects are working in the municipal sector, in particular in offices, to the applause of a public keen to thrill to the shock of the new.

This *zeitgeistlichkeit* will wash away the petticoats of history to which many architects cling, and toast the past — especially the recent past — only in order to celebrate the future.

It might be that the work is *avant-garde,* especially in the context of similar *fin-et-commencement-de-siècle* movements such as the Secessionists, Suprematists and Constructivists whose originality provided the foundation for so much of the New Modern movement.

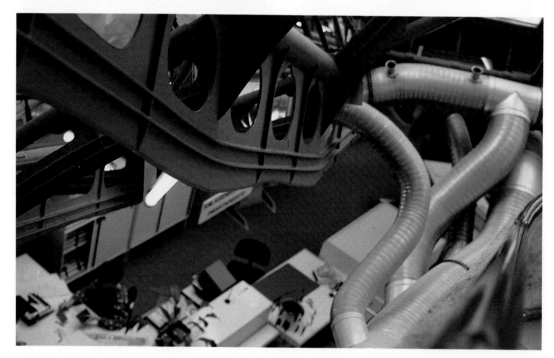

Central Bank Vienna, Austria
The interior is marked by a compilation of
surfaces, ducts, inclined columns, a folded plate
facade and twisted walls. A huge hand animates
the central banking hall and points to the higher
offices and conference rooms.
ARCHITECT: Gunther Domenig, Vienna, Austria

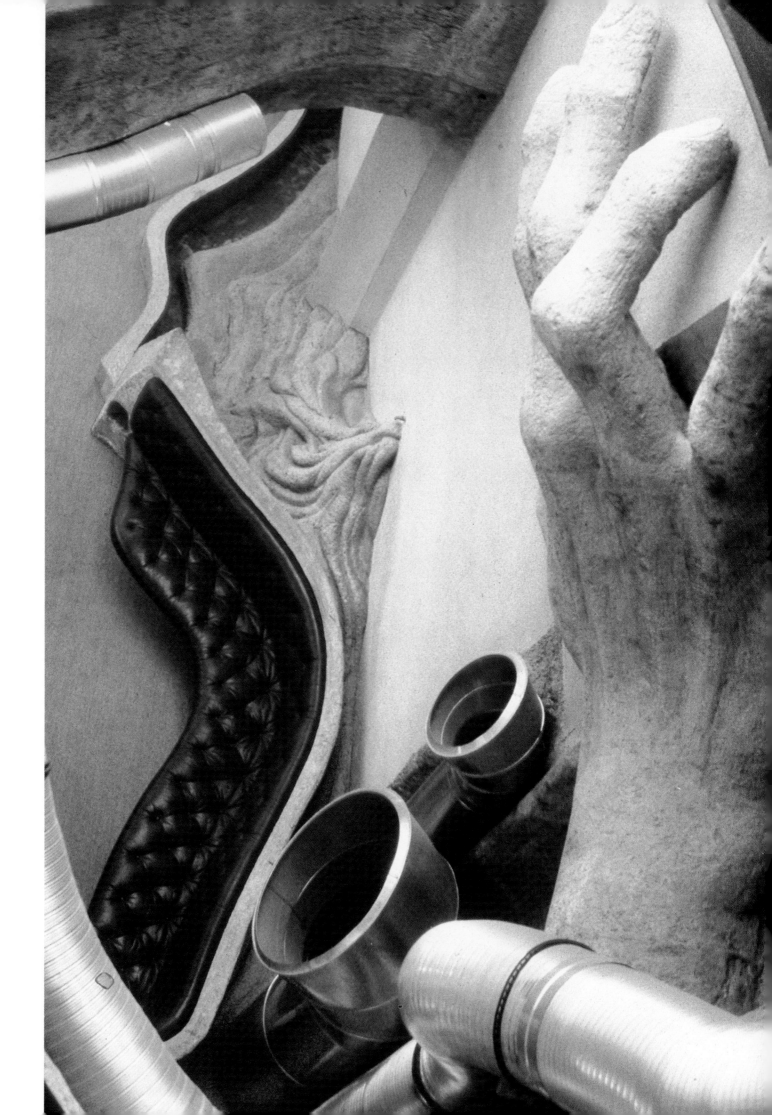

Falkestrasse 6, Vienna, Austria

The conference room in this law firm office sits under a folded plate canopy which is in turn supported by steel trusses and curved glazed panels. The whole assembly is spliced into and above the existing roof of an historic city building. The fractured assembly of ceiling canopy and structure casts a collage of shadows onto the surrounding walls and across the floors. The threshold between conference room and interior balcony on the terraced stairway is marked by a circle of neon, perhaps the only complete geometrical figure in the buildings composition.

ARCHITECT: Coop Himmelblau, Vienna, Austria

Falkestrasse 6 continued over page

Falkestrasse 6, Vienna, Austria
The partition walls to the street side combine a
structural transformation of the original roof
construction and the introduction of new
materials in order to free and functionalize the
spaces. The combination of inclined planes,
layered office surfaces, relatively modest
furniture and fractured structural figures
combine to create a complex interior which is
homogenized by a monochromatic surface
finish.
ARCHITECT: Coop Himmelblau, Vienna, Austria

Falkestrasse 6 continued

Helical Bar Properties, London, England
The small reception area has a wide palette of materials including glass, terracotta, light ash timberwork, leather and steel. The circular theme is reinforced by a specially designed circular rug.
ARCHITECT: McColl, London, England

Ridgway Associates, Los Angeles, California, USA

A combination of corrugated galvanized steel cladding, white plastered surfaces and modest timber doors provide an unusual combination of materials against a ceiling of exposed concrete and steel structure services and lighting.

ARCHITECT: Ridgway Associates, Los Angeles, California, USA

**Offices for Gary Withers at Imagination HQ,
London, England**

In contrast to the light, white steel and masonry
atrium space of the main offices, Gary Wither's
own two-tier office is busy with artifact and
artworks, (including a grand piano). A
spiral staircase links the levels and a roof terrace
commands views of London.

ARCHITECT: Gary Withers with Herron Associates,
London, England

Nave Rosa, Mercabarna, Barcelona, Spain
A broken circular blockwork screen reveals a
helical stair, apparently supported on a tall palm
that carries the eye from the entrance area to the
administration section above.
ARCHITECT: Alfredo Arribas Arquitectos
Associados, Barcelona, Spain

Chiat Day Advertising, London, England

There is rarely a good building without a good
client. Generally, clients will insist on the status
quo of mediocrity in order to insure against the
risk of speculative commercial failure. In the
context of so much ordinariness it is good to find
a client with the creative generosity of Chiat Day
and an architect of the quality of Stephano de
Martino. The product is an interior office project
of richness, energy, wit and dynamic, achieved
by a careful and eccentric choice of materials laid
over a structural geometry, all of which is
founded on a strong theoretical base.

ARCHITECT: Stephano de Martino, London,
England

Chiat Day continued

Morla Design Offices, San Francisco, California, USA

Jennifer Morla's own offices accommodate a design vocabulary that finds an integrity in the relationships of opposites. Texture, grain, surface and matrials ranging through rubber, stone, glass and plaster are counterpointed and juxtaposed to create an office of calm intrigue.

ARCHITECT: Jennifer Morla and Kepa Askenasy, Morla Associates, San Francisco, California, USA

Interventionist

Many office developments arise from the fitting out of an existing shell and core building. An architect working for the speculative developer will provide a type of multi-layered serviced shed comprising structure, services and fabric, but nothing else.

Once the shell and core have been let and a new client brings a specificity of function to bear upon the passive envelope, an opportunity arises for a powerful intervention, with the new insertion displaying its personality against an often uninspiring three-dimensional gridded box.

Another group of interventionist interiors occurs with the opportunity to provide a new use for an old building that is characterized by an architectural muscularity strong enough to withstand a radical insertion. In these instances, counterpoint and juxtaposition create an architectural dynamic of engaging originality. Architects and clients brave enough to embark on these adventures have a modern history of contemporary installationist art by which to be inspired.

In further examples, the host building is touched very lightly by the intervention, the quality of the minimalism in itself being enough to provide a profound characterization of the new place.

▼

▼

▼

Banque Bruxelles Lambert, Lausanne, Switzerland

The penetrating landscapes of Lausanne are recalled in the design of the bank's interiors – mountains, snow and lakes. To create a coherent whole where light, space, definition and texture are unified, a special unit was developed which consists of a row of ceiling lights hidden by layers of hanging silk threads that diffuse light while creating a misty transparency.

ARCHITECT: Emilio Ambasz & Associates, New York City, New York, USA

Banque Bruxelles Lambert Lausanne continued over page

Banque Bruxelles Lambert Lausanne continued

Banque Bruxelles Lambert, New York City, New York, USA
'New York' evokes images of tall buildings. Tall buildings hide other tall buildings and there is hardly enough open space to give a decent perspective of their façades. This design provides that perspective within the bank's offices by 'opening its windows' and making the walls 'transparent'.

ARCHITECT: Emilio Ambasz & Associates, New York City, New York, USA

Banque Bruxelles Lambert New York continued

Subterania, London, England

Subterania is a live music venue located beneath the elevated section of a London motorway. The motorway, supported by four vast concrete stanchions, acts as a canopy for a large, box-like internal space. A steel-framed gallery was constructed in the central part of this volume and the key facilities were arranged in a way which emphasized both stanchions and the underside of the concrete slabs which form the motorway carriages. Internally the stanchions were sandblasted and new openings were carved through them at strategic intervals. The choice of finishes was largely influenced by acoustic considerations and the requirement to withstand uncompromising use by the patrons. Materials included rubber slabs and ceramic tiles for the floors and bonded plaster and steel sheets to the walls. The lighting scheme combines proprietary fluorescent fittings clad in coloured jets with small tungsten lamps normally used as signal lamps in motor vehicles.

ARCHITECT: Madigan & Donald, London, England

Fielden Clegg Offices, Bath, Avon, England
The rooflit offices bring old and new together
through a pair of structural trees that neighbour
the principal staircase. An industrial vocabulary
in the detailing of balustrades and staircase
elements recalls earlier uses through the use of a
contemporary architectural language.
ARCHITECT: Fielden Clegg, Bath, Avon, Somerset

ITN Offices, London, England
Frameless glazed screens separate the top floor offices of the ITN building from the toplit atrium. With the structure and fabric unseparated and all in white, the interior has an homogeneity and lack of architectural hierarchy, leaving staff, furniture and office functions to express their personality against a passive and neutral background.
ARCHITECT: Foster Associates, London, England

Davis Ireland Smith Grey, London, England
The offices of this advertizing agency are housed in a listed building in Covent Garden. The mirrored ceiling, operating theatre light fittings and 'psychiatrist's couch' reception seating make oblique references to the agency's medical clientele. Polished oak floors, painted canvas wall panels, rosewood veneer furniture and lacquered steel metalwork all feature throughout.

ARCHITECT: Paul Mullins Associates, London, England

Lansdowne House, London, England
A series of arched headed openings establishes a strong perspective to the central circulation space. The geometry in proportion of these spaces is powerful enough to do without excess ornament decoration and colour.
ARCHITECT: Chapman Taylor Partners, London, England

Solid State Logic Headquarters, Stonesfield, Oxfordshire, England
A small spiral staircase doubles to provide a light gun into the lower floors. The precise composition of interrelated objects and furniture animates a simple yet engaging interior.
ARCHITECT: D. Clelland & E. Parry, London, England

Peat Marwick Thorne, Richmond Hill, Ontario, Canada

The aim was to create an image conscious public reception area with efficient office space and staff areas. The floorplate is divided into four quadrants, with the elevator lobby/reception core acting as a central axis for all traffic. The progression of spaces relates to the actual public/private function of the area. Glazing details punctuate the spatial relationships – as a canopy over the boardroom entry areas, as a blade across the reception wall and as a detail on the reception desk. The boardroom was designed to focus presentation and public meetings with large corporate clients. The etched glass wall provides partial visual and light link to reception area. The purple tone is used throughout in pattern and texture. The materials are used in a progressive manner and add traditional character to this space.

ARCHITECT: Inger Bartlett & Associates, Toronto, Ontario, Canada

**Financial Guaranty Insurance
Company, New York City, New York, USA**
A combination of daylight, artificial light,
hanging translucent screens and reflection
provides an office interior that is veiled from the
outside world and revealed to the imagination.
Flexibility is achieved by an open-office
environment into which self-contained modular
work units are inserted. Glass walls admit
abundant natural light and foster a sense of
community, as everyone can see each other. By
clustering the units in different ways, various
work organizations can be accommodated. The
corridor between the units becomes a
communal space rather than merely circulation.
ARCHITECT: Emilio Ambasz, New York City, New
York, USA

Lloyd Northover, London, England

The main reception space has been refurbished to give three areas within the main walkway where impromptu meetings can be held, thus transforming a lobby into a working area. Finely detailed timber, steel and glass contrast to the existing circular support columns. A continuous folded screen of translucent panels divides the entrance area from the office beyond.

ARCHITECT: Lloyd Northover, London, England

Marketplace, London, England

These design offices and studios are housed in a refurbished Victorian tea warehouse; as much existing structure and fabric was reused as possible, with high tech insertions where necessary. Additions include a four storey triangular side extension and a rooftop pavilion. A rich but limited palette was used to the new elements and new window frames on old and new parts of the building used as a unifying feature. Lightweight structures were used for the additions to complement the heavy engineering of the existing masonry structure.

ARCHITECT: Weston Williamson, London, England

Banque Bruxelles Lambert, Milan, Italy
The Neoclassical interior of this 19th century building has been restored and carefully painted to subdue some of the more Baroque detailing. In order to intensify the counterpoint between the new architectural design and the found setting, the simple device of framing the new areas with a conceptual black line was used to help define the interface between new and old. An elegant touch of irony comes from the staircase, balustrade and handrail, an essay in contemporary mannerism.
ARCHITECT: Emilio Ambasz, New York City, New York, USA

Latham & Watkins Law Offices, Los Angeles, California, USA

The headquarter offices of this nationwide law firm are located on nine floors of a major downtown skyscraper. The building's geometric character consists of a 'field' of rotating squares and a distinct lack of 90° angles. To complement the faceted nature of the floor plate, the building's geometry was utilized as a design tool: the result has such major elements as the entries into the attorneys' offices falling precisely at regular points on the curving grid. To offset this rigid geometry, a secondary geometry was introduced. A series of curves radiating from points within the building's matrix softens the space and creates a clear direction for circulation.

ARCHITECT: Skidmore, Owings & Merrill, Los Angeles, California, USA

MI Group, London, England

Translucent glazed screens to go with glass and veneered doors frame the new Wimbledon offices of the MI Group. The entrance area is marked out in a circle of terrazzo and the upper floors are furnished with leather, chrome and walnut veneer.

ARCHITECT: The Design Solution, London, England

Origin III, Tokyo, Japan
The vaulted hallway is lit by a cluster of lights that mark the principal door. At a higher level, a series of thin rectangular windows illuminates the vaulted ceiling. The composition of space, light and materials has a certain religiosity and formality.
ARCHITECT: Shin Takamatsu, Kyoto, Japan

Winchester Offices, Winchester, Hampshire, England

The inhabited roof provides an opportunity for characterization. Conventional roof trusses have been remodelled to amplify the geometries while gridded glazed screens allow daylight from roof windows into the heart of the building.

ARCHITECT: Plinke Leaman Browning, London, England

Haworth Showroom, Chicago, Illinois, USA
Located in a classic bay concrete warehouse, the
showroom exploits the structural system to
create the ordered, passive environment
considered by the client as the optimum
background for product display. Mechanical,
electrical and fireproofing systems all reinforce
the geometric grid and the steel curtain wall
recalls industrial construction. Transposed
against the grid a random assemblage of
industrial outbuildings establishes a metaphor of
the steel industry – a symbol of Haworth's
midwestern manufacturing product.
ARCHITECT: Tigerman McCurry, Chicago, Illinois,
USA

**Hybrid Arts Qualitative Research Center,
Culver City, California, USA**
The timber pots and trusswork of the original
building shell (a plastics factory) stand
undisguised, juxtaposed with glazed panels and
rooflights and painted frames to produce an
architectural metaphor which refers to the name
of the building's new function. The Qualitative
Research Center is housed in the overall project.
ARCHITECT: Eric Owen Moss, Culver City,
California, USA

BP Exploration Inc., Houston, Texas, USA
Pairs of columns provide pencils of colour to
mark the threshold of the offices. The plain walls
and floor coverings provide an appropriate foil to
the downlighting and column clusters.
ARCHITECT: Gensler Associates, San Francisco,
California, USA

Gary Group, Culver City, California, USA

This adventurous building for PR consultants has been designed, according to the architect, as a picaresque novel, that is, a series of disparate adventures involving the same cast of characters. Like the novel, it can be opened and read at any point. Therefore, it has two entrances. One is cut from an almost free standing concrete block which rests on 'C' shaped steel ribs implanted in an adjoining wall. The second entrance is cut into a wall embellished with chains, wires, pipes, block planters and flowers. Inside the building, work stations are arranged within a cruciform plan. At the centre of the plan is a pool, open to the sky watered by steel shower heads which drop the water through a marble chute.

ARCHITECT: Eric Owen Moss, Culver City, California, USA

The Gary Group continued over page

The Gary Group continued

Gary Group, Culver City, California, USA

A conference area rotates, by complex overlapping geometries, around a steel table located beneath a truncated conical steel-clad roof window. At the cross axis, a fountain in marble and steel cools the small vestibule that gives way to private office suites.

ARCHITECT: Eric Owen Moss, Culver City, California, USA

Goalen Group Offices, Culver City, California, USA

The offices of a film production company are marked in the centre of the composition by a drum that rises through the roof to embrace a pair of inclined rooflights. The geometry of the intervention collides with the green structure of an original warehouse into which are woven the brown and grey partitions of the new office.

ARCHITECT: Eric Owen Moss, Culver City, California, USA

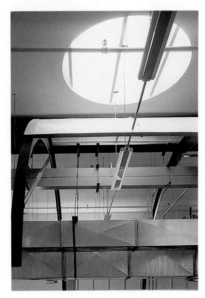

Scott Mednick Associates, Culver City, California, USA

The offices for this design firm specializing in video graphics centre on a causeway anchored at the west end by an exercise room and on the east end by a stairwell. The causeway perimeter is defined by fully enclosed offices on the south and partially enclosed work areas to the north. The causeway itself follows an original line of wood post supports and connecting beams running the length of the space. Steel angles bolted to both sides of the wood beams form a precise organizational reference line to which all additional components conform.

ARCHITECT: Eric Owen Moss, Culver City, California, USA

Scott Mednick Associates continued over page

Scott Mednick Associates, continued

Scott Mednick Associates, Culver City, California, USA

A second line of private offices runs parallel to the causeway with three circulation links to the main walk. These three circulation intersections are defined by stiffening pairs of steel ribs with tubular struts and fastening ribbed acrylic sheets over the ribs. Domed skylights are positioned above the acrylic sheets. The interior roof of the exercise room at the west end of the walk is a wood deck accessed by stairs on either side of the exercise room. From the platform a stair provides service access to the roof. At the opposite end, the central walk connects with two floors of executive offices and conference space.

ARCHITECT: Eric Owen Moss, Culver City, California, USA

Lindblade Tower, Culver City, California, USA

The former warehouse at the corner of Ince and Lindblade Boulevard has been converted to two uses: film company offices and Moss's own studios. A partially clad tower gives light to mark the entrance space that gives way to a clear flexible office area underneath the restored roof truss structure. At the centre of the composition, a small garden, or outdoor room, is revealed from an up and over glazed door to provide air, light and shade.

ARCHITECT: Eric Owen Moss, Culver City, California, USA

Paramount Laundry, Culver City, California, USA

The former laundry building has been converted to design and architecture offices. The principal façade retains most of the mid-century architectural elements, sitting behind a line of clay pipe columns that act as icons to the new function. Behind the façade, a new and radical intervention portrays the spirit of the new use against fragments of old structures and recycled fabric.

ARCHITECT: Eric Owen Moss, Culver City, California, USA

Paramount Laundry continued over page

Qualitative Research Center, Culver City, California, USA

The offices of the Qualitative Research Corporation, a consumer affairs research group, are housed in an old warehouse remodelled in 1988, with northeast oriented saw-tooth skylights and wood truss supported roof. There are no perimeter windows. The programme combines open and closed office space for both business activity and graphic design, two conference rooms, kitchen, and a library.
ARCHITECT: Eric Owen Moss, Culver City, California, USA

The Qualitative Research Center continued

Qualitative Research Center, Culver City, California, USA

The library is the conceptual center of the project. Pentagonal in plan, each external side faces a particular programme use. The pentagon is modified both in plan and section to accommodate requirements and existing construction. The walls splay outward gathering a maximum of natural light as they intersect the existing saw-tooth roof. A cold-rolled steel table cantilevers from an existing post in the room, and cold-rolled steel shelves hang from two walls. All furniture is designed specifically for the space. Built-in counters are lacquered strand board. One desk for the QRC lobby is cold-rolled steel and glass, the other vertical grain fir and cold-rolled steel.

ARCHITECT: Eric Owen Moss, Culver City, California, USA

The Qualitative Research Center continued

Index of Projects

Directory of Practising Architects

This directory lists the addresses of architects in current practice. While every effort has been made to ensure that this list was correct at the time of going to press, subsequent changes in address or status are beyond the publishers' remit.

Allies & Morrison Architects
54 Newman Street, London WIP 3PG, England
PROJECTS: The Clove Building 120–1; The Scott Howard Building 122–3

Emilio Ambasz & Associates
636 Broadway, New York City, New York 10012 USA
PROJECTS: Banque Bruxelles Lambert Lausanne 164–5; Banque Bruxelles Lambert Milan 186–7; Banque Bruxelles Lambert New York 167–9; Financial Guaranty Insurance Company 180

Alfredo Arribas Arquitectos Associados
Balmes 345, 1 2, 08006 Barcelona, Spain
PROJECT: Nave Rosa 154–5

Beyer Blinder Belle
41 East 11th Street, New York City, New York 100003, USA
PROJECT: Della Femina McNamee Inc. 116–7

Chapman Taylor Partners
96 Kensington High Street, London W8 4SG, England
PROJECT: Lansdowne House 176

Chassay Architects
90 Westbourne Terrace, London W2 6QE, England
PROJECT: The Fitzpatrick Building 136–7

Coop Himmelblau
Sellerstätte 16/11a, A 1010 Vienna, Austria
PROJECT: Falkestrasse 6 146–8

Crabtree Hall Associates
70 Crabtree Lane, London SW6 6LT, England
PROJECT: F1 Group 93

DY Davies Associates
36 Paradise Road, Richmond, Surrey TW9 1SE, England
PROJECT: 3 Stratford Place 34–5

Alan Dehar Associates
85 Willow Street, New Haven, Connecticut 06511, USA
PROJECT: Romantic Languages Building, Yale 83

The Design Solution
20 Kingly Court, London W1R 5LE, England
PROJECTS: Heron International 29; M1 Group 190; Seward Properties 36

Ellerbe Becket Inc.
1 Appletree Square, Minneapolis, Minnesota 55425, USA and
605 West 47th Street, Kansas City, Missouri 64112, USA and
636 Broadway, New York City, New York 10012, USA
PROJECTS: Deloitte & Touche 108–11; Own Offices Kansas City 112–5; Own Offices St Paul 32–3

Fielden Clegg Design
Bath Brewery, Tollbridge Road, Bath BA1 7DE, Avon, England
PROJECT: Own Offices 172

Fitzroy Robinson Partnership
77 Portland Place, London W1N 4EP, England
PROJECT: Mitsui Trust & Banking 46

Foster Associates
Riverside Three, Albert Wharf, 22 Heston Road, London SW11 4AN, England
PROJECTS: Century Tower 139–141; ITN 173; Willis, Faber & Dumas 9, 87

Phillippe Gazeau
17 rue Froment, 7501 Paris, France
PROJECTS: Industrial Kitchen 76; with Marc Beri: Municipal Nursery 74–5

Gensler Associates
550 Kearney Street, San Francisco, California 94108, USA
PROJECTS: American Express Bank 92; BP Exploration 197; Enron Corporation 77; Perkins Coie 25

Michael Graves Architect
341 Nassau Street, Princeton, New Jersey 08540, USA
PROJECT: Crown Corporate Building 26

Hampshire County Architects Department
Three Minsters House, 76 High Street, Winchester SO23 8UL, Hampshire, England
PROJECTS: Berrywood County Primary School 15; Town End House 134

Harper Mackay
36–7 Charterhouse Square, London EC1M 6EA, England
PROJECT: Delaney Fletcher Slaymaker Delaney Bozell 29

Herman Hertzberger
Vossiusstraat 3, 1071 CD Amsterdam, Netherlands
PROJECT: Centraal Beheer 13

T.L. Horton Design Inc.
11120 Grader Street, Dallas, Texas 75238, USA
PROJECT: Own Offices 88–90

Imagination Design & Communication
25 Store Street, South Crescent, London WC1E 7BL, England
PROJECTS: Gary Witherrs Office at Imagination 152–3; Own Offices 103–4

Inger Bartlett & Associates
2a Gibson Avenue, Toronto, Ontario M5R 1TS, Canada
PROJECT: Cavelti Capital 24; Peat Marwick Thorne 178–9; Royal Bank Toronto 85

Jestico + Whiles Architects
14 Stephenson Way, London NW1 2HD, England
PROJECTS: Ove Arup & Partners 102–3; Own Offices 52–3; Policy Studies Institute 100–1

Jung Brannen Associates Inc.
177 Milk Street, Boston, Massachusetts 02109, USA
PROJECT: Massachusetts Financial Services Company 20–1

Kisho Kurakawa Architect & Associates
11th Floor, Aoyama Building, 2–3 Kita Aoyama I-chome, Toshima-ku 170, Tokyo, Japan
PROJECTS: Heian Kojimachi 63; Wacoal Kojimachi 60–

Larson Associates
542 South Dearborn, Chicago, Illinois 60605, USA
PROJECT: Aon Corporation 65

Peter Leonard Associates Ltd
55 Kings Road, London SW10 0SZ, England
PROJECT: 3i 59

Lloyd Northover
8 Smarts Place, London WC2B 5LW, England
PROJECT: Own Offices 182–3

Madigan & Donald
2 Primrose Mews, Sharpeshall Street, London NW1 8YW, England
PROJECT: Subterania 170–1

P. Michael Marino
Marino Newman Architects, 434 Sixth Avenue, 6th Floor, New York City, New York 10011, USA
PROJECT: afa Asset Services 54–5

Stephano de Martino
26 Roupell Street, London SE1 8TB, England
PROJECT: Chiat Day Advertising 17, 156–9

Manser Associates
Bridge Studies, Hammersmith Bridge, London W6 9DA, England
PROJECT: Bridge Studios 132–3

McColl Group International
64 Wigmore Street, London W1H 9DJ, England
PROJECTS: Hampton House 78; Helical Bar Properties 150; Nikko Securities Headquarters 28; Queen Anne Building 31

Morla Design
463 Bryant Street, San Francisco, California 94107, USA
PROJECT: Own Offices 160–1

Eric Owen Moss
3964 Ince Boulevar, Culver City, California 90232, USA
PROJECTS: The Gary Group 198–201; The Goalen Group 202–3; Hybrid Arts Qualitative Research Center 196; Lindblade Tower 210–11; Paramount Laundry 212–7; Scott Mednick Associates 204–9; Qualitative Research Center 218–221

Paul Mullins
44–6 Scrutton Street, London EC2A 4HH, England
PROJECTS: Davis Ireland Smith Grey 174–5; DIN 50–1

Munkenbeck & Marshall
113–7 Farringdon Road, London EC1 3BT, England
PROJECT: Jessica Square 176–9

Nicoll Russell Studios
Westfield Road, Broughty Fields, Dundee DDS 1ED, Scotland
PROJECT: TSB Bank 47

ORMS
1 Pine Street, London EC1R 0JH, England
PROJECTS: NEXT HQ 80–82; Own Offices 106–7

Pei Cobb Freed & Partners
600 Madison Avenue, New York City, New York 10022, USA
PROJECT: Bank of China 138

Cesar Pelli Associates
1056 Chapel Street, New Haven, Connecticut 06511, USA
PROJECT: Battery Park Financial Center 130–1

Alan Phillips Associates
50 Cambridge Road, Brighton BN3 1DF, East Sussex, England
PROJECT: Trattoria Capri 135

RSCG Conran Design Ltd
The Clove Building, 4 Maguire Street, London
SE1 2NQ, England
PROJECT: Butlers Wharf Development Corporation

Ridgway Associates
414 Boyd Street, Los Angeles, California 90013, USA
PROJECT: Own Offices 151

Rock Townsend
35 Alfred Place, London WC1E 7DP, England
PROJECT: IBM Midlands 56–7

Richard Rogers Partnership
Thames Wharf Studios, Rainsville Road, London
W6 9HA, England
PROJECT: The Lloyds Building 68–9

David Schwarz Architectural Services
1133 Connecticut Avenue NW, Suite 800, Washington
DC 20036, USA
PROJECT: Cook-Fort Worth Children's Hospital 16

Harry Seidler & Associates
2 Glen Street, Milson's Pont, New South Wales 2061,
Australia
PROJECT: Capita Centre 64; Grosvenor Place 72–3;
The Riverside Centre 91; Shell House 70–1

Shin Takamatsu Associates
38–4 Jobogalin-cho, Takeda, Fushimi-ku, Tokyo,
Japan
PROJECT: Origins III 191

Skidmore, Owings & Merrill
220 East 42nd Street, New York City, New York 10017,
USA and
33 West Munro Street, Chicago, Illinois 60603, USA

and
725 South Figuerada Street, Los Angeles, California
90017, USA and
333 Bush Street, San Francisco, California 94104, USA
and
Devonshire House, Mayfair Place, London W1X 5FP,
England
PROJECTS: The Broadgate Development 14; Kirkland
& Ellis 86; Latham & Watkins 188–9; Herman Miller
118–9; 505 Montgomery 27; Pacific Bell 67; Pacific
Telesis 38–9; South East Bank 142

The Switzer Group Inc.
302 Broadway, New York City, New York 10010, USA
PROJECT: Gilliam & Company 22–3

Thomas Brent Associates
222 Tower Bridge Road, London SE1 2UP, England
PROJECT: London Dock House 30

Tigerman McCurry
444 North Wells Street, Chicago, Illinois 60610, USA
PROJECT: Haworth Showroom 194–5

Troughton McAslan
202 Kensington Church Street, London W8 4BP,
England
PROJECT: Design House 58

Vignelli Associates
475 Tenth Avenue, New York City, New York 10018,
USA
PROJECTS: Poltrona Frau 96–8; Own Offices 94–5

Weston Williams
10 Burlington Lodge Studios, Rigault Road, London
SW6 4JJ, England
PROJECTS: Marketplace 184–5; A.J. Vines 99

Photographic Acknowledgements

AA = Architectural Association.

p 9 **Peter Tunison/AA**; p 10 **A.M. Minchin/AA**; p 11 **Bill Chiatkin/AA**; p 12 **Victor Lim/AA**; p 14 **Tony Weller/AA**; p 15 **Joe Low/AA**; p 16 top: **Peter Cook/AA**; bottom **Hedrich-Blessing**; p 17 **Sophie de Martino**; p 20–1 **Nick Wheeler**; p 22–3 **Mark Ross**; p 24 **David Whittaker**; p 25 **Peter Aaron/Esto Photographics**; p 26 **Tim Hursley**; p 27 **Jane Lidz**; p 28 **McColl Group International**; p 29 **Michael Caldwell**; p 30 **Tony Weller/AA**; p 31 **McColl Group International**; p 32–3 **Peter Aaron/Esto Photographics**; p 34–5 **E.C. Dickson/Holloway White Allom**; p 36–7 **Jon O'Brien**; p 38–9 **Christopher Irion**; p 40–1 **Ezra Stoller/Esto Photographics**; p 44–5 **Steve Reynolds**; p 46 **Ian Knaggs**; p 47 **Alistair Hunter**; p 50–1 **Jon O'Brien**; p 52 top: **Michael Heffernan**; bottom **Paul Ratigan**; p 53 **Paul Ratigan**; p 54 **Paul Warchol**; p 56–7 **Richard Bryant**; p 58 **Peter Cook**; p 59 **Nick Clark/Peter Leonard Associates**; p 60–3 **Tomio Ohashi**; p 64 **Harry Seidler & Associates**; p 65 **Nick Merrick/Hedrich-Blessing**; p 66 **Pawson Silvestrin/AA**; p 67 **William Helsel**; p 68 **Peter Cook/AA**; p 69 **P. Barnett/AA**; p 70–3 **Harry Seidler & Associates**; p 74–6 **J.M. Monthiers**; p 77 **Nick Merrick/Hedrich-Blessing**; p 78 **McColl Group International**; p 79 **Dennis Gilbert**; p 80–2 **Peter Cook/Richard Bryant**; p 83 **Robert Perron**; p 84 **Lio Malka/AA**; p 85 **David Whittaker**; p 86 **Hedrich-Blessing**; p 87 **Peter Tunison/AA**; p 88–90 **Joe C. Aker**; p 91 **Harry Seidler & Associates**; p 92 **Chas McGrath**; p 93 **Crabtree Hall**; p 94–5 **Luca Vignelli**; p 95 bottom right: **Mario Carrieri**; p 96–8 **Antonia Mulas**; p 99 **Weston Williamson**; p 100–1 **Matthew Weinreb**; p 102–3 **John Peck/Jo Reid**; p 104–5 **Terry Hope at Imagination**; p 106–7 **Peter Cook**; p 108–11 **Dan Cornish/Chuck Choi**; p 112–5 **Assassi Productions**; p 116–7 **Roy J. Wright**; p 118–9 **Hedrich-Blessing**; p 120–3 **Peter Cook**; p 124–5 **Valerie Bennett/AA**; p 126–9 **Dennis Gilbert**; p 130–1 **S.D. & A.J. Margolis/AA**; p 132–3 **Manser Associates**; p 134 **Joe Low/AA**; p 135 **Allan Phillips**; p 136–7 **Horst Kola**; p 138 **John Lau/AA**; p 139–141 **Sophie Hicks/AA**; p 144–5 **Peter Cook/AA**; p 146–9 **Gerald Zugmann**; p 150 **McColl Group International**; p 151 **Ridgway Associates**; p 152–3 **Tony Harris at Imagination**; p 154–5 **Javier Mariscal**; p 156–9 **Sophie de Martino**; p 160–1 **Jennifer Morla**; p 164–6 **Santi Caleca**; p 167–9 **Paul Warchol**; p 170–1 **David George**; p 172 **Tony Weller/AA**; p 173 **ITN/AA**; p 174–5 **Peter Cook**; p 176 **Leighton Gibbins**; p 177 **Barry Capper/AA**; p 178–9 **David Whittaker**; p 180–1 **Paul Warchol**; p 182–5 **Peter Cook**; p 186–7 **Santi Caleca**; p 188–9 **Nick Merrick/Hedrich-Blessing**; p 190 **Michael Caldwell**; p 191 **Katsuaki Furidate**; p 192–3 **Joe Low/AA**; p 194–5 **Tim Hursley**; p 196 **Grant Mudford**; p 197 **IRA Montgomery**; p 198–203 **Tom Bonner**; p 204–9 **Grant Mudford**; p 210–12 **Alex Vertikoff**; p 213 **Frank Jackson**; p 214–5 **Berger/Conser**; p.216–7 **Alex Vertikoff**; p 218–221 **Grant Mudford**.

Many thanks to Valerie Bennett of the Architectural Association.